A *season* of *sundays*

*Images of the 2021 Gaelic Games year by the Sportsfile team
of photographers, with text by Alan Milton*

An official GAA publication, published by Sportsfile

CARROLL'S
EST. 1979
of Tullamore

Season provided a sense of hope

The 2021 GAA season gave a new sense of hope to the nation during the pandemic because the GAA is, for so many, a sense of home and familiarity. With the country and the games returning to a 'new normal' we saw those who were apart for so long coming together again, with spirits raised to enjoy those little things like the thrill of a penalty or the sound of a puck. It was a sign of hope that we will get there.

The return of the championship season to its summer schedule was anticipated like never before. As we know, the major trophies went to Limerick and Tyrone, with the awesome Treaty side taking the Liam MacCarthy Cup for the third time in four years and the Red Hands surprising the pundits by winning the Sam Maguire Cup for the first time in 13 years.

In Offaly, we also took pride watching our under-20 footballers become All-Ireland champions at this grade, a memorable day for the county which we at Carroll's support. Indeed, it was a year of progress for the Faithful County with the senior footballers and hurlers earning promotion in their respective leagues and the hurlers winning the Christy Ring Cup.

We are humbled with the continued support we receive from our local community in Tullamore and, of course, our customers nationwide. When choosing Carroll's of Tullamore, not only will you enjoy the benefits of over 40 years of crafting excellence but you will also be contributing to a proud Irish business, as we continue to take our time slow-cooking all our meats to perfection, producing delicious ham, award-winning poultry and succulent beef.

Finally, 2021 marked an important year for Carroll's as we celebrated 30 years supporting Offaly GAA. We are proud to have had the Offaly jersey carrying the Carroll's logo since 1991, along with the heritage and community that it stands for.

We hope you enjoy this edition of *A Season of Sundays* as much as we always do, and are excited to see what next year's GAA season brings.

– THE CARROLL'S OF TULLAMORE TEAM

Published by:
SPORTSFILE
Patterson House, 14 South Circular Road
Portobello, Dublin 8, D08 T3FK, Ireland
www.sportsfile.com

Photographs:
Copyright © 2021 Sportsfile

Text:
Alan Milton

Editing:
Eddie Longworth

Quotations research:
Seán Creedon

Design:
The Design Gang, Tralee

Colour reproduction:
Mark McGrath

Printing / Binding production:
PB Print Solutions

The Sportsfile photographic team:

Ben McShane

Brendan Moran

Dáire Brennan

David Fitzgerald

Diarmuid Greene

Eóin Noonan

Harry Murphy

Matt Browne

Piaras Ó Mídheach

Ramsey Cardy

Ray McManus

Sam Barnes

Seb Daly

Stephen McCarthy

Without limiting the rights under copyright, this book is sold subject to the condition that it shall not, by way of trade or otherwise, be lent, resold, hired out, reproduced, stored in or introduced into a retrieval system, or transmitted, in any form or by any means (electronic, mechanical, photocopying, recording or otherwise), or otherwise circulated, without the publisher's prior consent, in any form other than that in which it is published and without a similar condition, including this condition, being imposed on the subsequent publisher.

ISBN: 978-1-905468-53-9

Any old prints query inspired 25 years documenting our national games

I was sitting at my desk in a small office in North Great Denmark Street in Dublin 25 years ago and the phone rang. "Hello. Is that you Raymond? Raymond Smith here."

He always called me by my proper name. No Ray with our Raymond. "Would you have any old prints lying around the darkroom floor? I got some from the *Independent* and need a few more."

I printed up a few and he arrived the next day at noon to collect them. Nice man and a great GAA writer our Raymond but even though many photos go unpublished, I still took exception to anyone thinking that "old prints lying around" could be acquired so casually and therefore sought a solution.

The solution, of course, was to publish a book. A call to my good friend Peadar Staunton, a designer of note, prompted me to visit a number of bookshops and select the format that would show Gaelic games pictures at their best.

Ultimately I decided on a large-format coffee table book and since that day I have had the pleasure of publishing *A Season of*

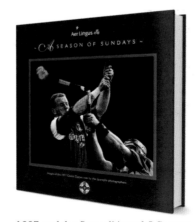

1997 and the first edition of *A Season of Sundays* appears on book shelves with a cover featuring the iconic image of Limerick's teak-tough corner back, Stephen McDonagh, testing the strength of some Tipperary ash

Sundays each year. The first edition featured the work of just five photographers while this one, our 25th, has 14. Great progress from my point of view but the progress from 'any old prints' to today's high-resolution digital files has been equally impressive.

Books of this calibre could not happen without some great people aside from the photographers, and here I think of Alan Milton who has written the words. The help and support of the aforementioned Peadar Staunton and indeed our sub editor Eddie Longworth and 'quotations research man' Seán Creedon are greatly appreciated.

Finally one very important supporter – the team sponsor. While we do not wear their name on our chests we do depend greatly on one of the GAA's longest-running sponsors – Carroll's of Tullamore. Thank you especially.

The return of crowds is the big bonus in slow return to normality

Lenár gcuid craobhacha idirchontae thart anois, tá sé in am duinn súil a chaitheamh siar ar bhliain thaitneamhach, dhúshlánach eile i saol an Chumainn agus muid ag cur fáilte roimh an bhfoilseachán iontach seo arís.

As the curtain comes down on another eventful year we have another edition of *A Season of Sundays* – the 25th in all – to look forward to.

For many GAA members and supporters it is an eagerly awaited addition to personal collections as moments – both big and small – are captured in Sportsfile's unique way.

No two GAA seasons are the same. From winners and losers, highlights, unforgettable examples of brilliance and everything in between, the unpredictability of it all is what keeps us coming back for more.

The beauty of this project really becomes apparent when you look back at past editions and marvel at the memories that jump off the pages, the ageing hairstyles and the dated playing gear.

The period of 2020–2021 will be referenced in years to come as one without compare. Last year we could be considered fortunate to get our games played, though the absence of supporters detracted somewhat from the experience of watching – and I'm sure playing in – the matches. Thankfully that was remedied to some extent this year and attendance figures crept up as the season wore on. And what a difference it made.

Larry McCarthy, second right, who became the 40th president of the GAA when he succeeded John Horan earlier this year, is among the handful of spectators in Darver, Co Louth in his first official visit to a match. A native of Cork, McCarthy lived in New York for 36 years and is the first overseas person to become GAA president. His first trophy presentation came after this Division 3B hurling league game between Louth and Fermanagh

Unlike 2020, the season also had a more familiar schedule with the leagues starting in spring before the championships got under way in the summer months.

Old foes Dublin and Kerry shared league honours in football and Galway and Kilkenny topped their respective tables in hurling and finished as joint winners.

Again in contrast to 2020, provincial championship shocks were in short supply. While the exploits of Cavan and Tipperary in winning the Ulster and Munster titles caught people's imaginations last year, some of the traditional powers reasserted themselves in 2021.

On the football front, the provincial titles went to Kerry, Dublin, Tyrone and Mayo, with the latter two counties claiming the Ulster and Connacht titles in Croke Park.

In hurling, Limerick's stock rose further when one of the comebacks of the year allowed them to reel in Tipperary in the Munster final while Kilkenny accounted for Dublin in the Leinster decider.

Attendances increased significantly at the semi-final stages and the return of the familiar Croke Park din – even with crowds around the 20,000 mark – added hugely to the atmosphere and sense of occasion for the hurling meetings of Waterford and Limerick and Kilkenny and Cork before Limerick and Cork advanced to a first All-Ireland final meeting.

Limerick then produced a first-half display for the ages in the final to seal their second consecutive Liam MacCarthy Cup success and third in four years.

Mayo's success in ending Dublin's six-year unbeaten run stood out as one of the performances of the season only to be rivalled by Tyrone's win over Kerry after the Ulster champions' well-documented challenges with Covid.

Tyrone also excelled on final day to end a 13-year wait for the Sam Maguire Cup and extend Mayo's wait by at least one more year.

However, the results tell only part of the story. More than ever, the games provided a welcome distraction and, as the season progressed, they provided a vehicle for direct engagement with members and supporters and restored the valued tradition of bringing people together.

It all served as a reminder of how important our games are to so many, and we are unlikely to take them for granted in the future.

Of course, in a year as challenging and as unusual as this you would expect to see images that would not normally be associated with the staging of our games. Empty stands, fist bumps, unusual vantage points, social distancing and face masks all feature in this year's edition for what we hope will be the last time.

As ever, the eagle-eyed Sportsfile photographers were there to capture these happenings and record them not only for us to savour, but as a historical record for future generations.

There are few intercounty league or championship fixtures from one end of the year to the other that are not covered by Ray McManus or one of his team.

Sportsfile's innate understanding of Cumann Lúthchleas Gael and our games provides them with unique opportunities to capture special moments, many of them away from the cut-and-thrust of the action between the white lines.

That they have been doing this for so long, not just for this publication, but on an almost daily basis for decades, means they have done the GAA a service that is worthy of acknowledgement. Similarly, I know the support of Carroll's of Tullamore is of vital importance to the project and I hope they derive great satisfaction from the successes enjoyed this year by the Offaly hurlers and the under-20 footballers – teams also supported by Carroll's.

I hope you enjoy this latest edition of *A Season of Sundays*. Congratulations to Ray, Anne and the entire Sportsfile team for extending a valued tradition by one more year.

Long may it continue.

Go n-éirí go geal libh.

LARRY MCCARTHY
UACHTARÁN CHUMANN LÚTHCHLEAS GAEL

8 Allianz Hurling League - TEG Cusack Park, Mullingar
Westmeath 1-16   Galway 5-34

Allianz Hurling League - Parnell Park, Dublin
Dublin 0-18   Kilkenny 1-20

2.

(1) Welcome back, we missed you. A late start is better than no start at all with the 2021 GAA season delayed until May 8th because of the prolonged lockdown in the country as the Government and the health service try to get to grips with the Covid pandemic. So, it's no surprise that Derek McNicholas gets a warm round of applause when leading the Westmeath team out for the very first game of the year. Alas, the reception on the field from the Galway visitors is not so welcoming

(2) The loneliness of the long-distance runner. Richie Hogan goes through an individual session in Parnell Park, a vignette that sets the tone for a frustrating year on the fringes for the former Hurler of the Year

8   Allianz Hurling League - LIT Gaelic Grounds, Limerick
Limerick 0-20   Tipperary 0-20

9   Allianz Hurling League - Corrigan Park, Belfast
Antrim 1-21   Clare 0-22

1.

2.

(1) The empty seats tell their own tale. The games are back but not
the fans – not yet anyway. Meanwhile, Limerick don a special
commemorative hooped jersey to mark the 100th anniversary of the
county's success in the 1921 All-Ireland and the first time the Liam
MacCarthy Cup was presented

(2) The Saffrons add a little spice to the league. Antrim, learning fast
under manager Darren Gleeson, record their first win over one of the
major hurling counties since 2012, turning over Clare despite the
best efforts of Tony Kelly. Here, Kelly strikes a free over the bar in his
11-point haul, the first of many huge tallies he would accumulate as
the year progresses

9 Allianz Hurling League - Chadwick's Wexford Park, Wexford
Wexford 4-17   Laois 0-10

Allianz Hurling League - Páirc Uí Chaoimh, Cork
Cork 5-22   Waterford 1-27

Allianz Hurling League - Páirc Tailteann, Navan
Meath 3-09   Offaly 3-25

1.

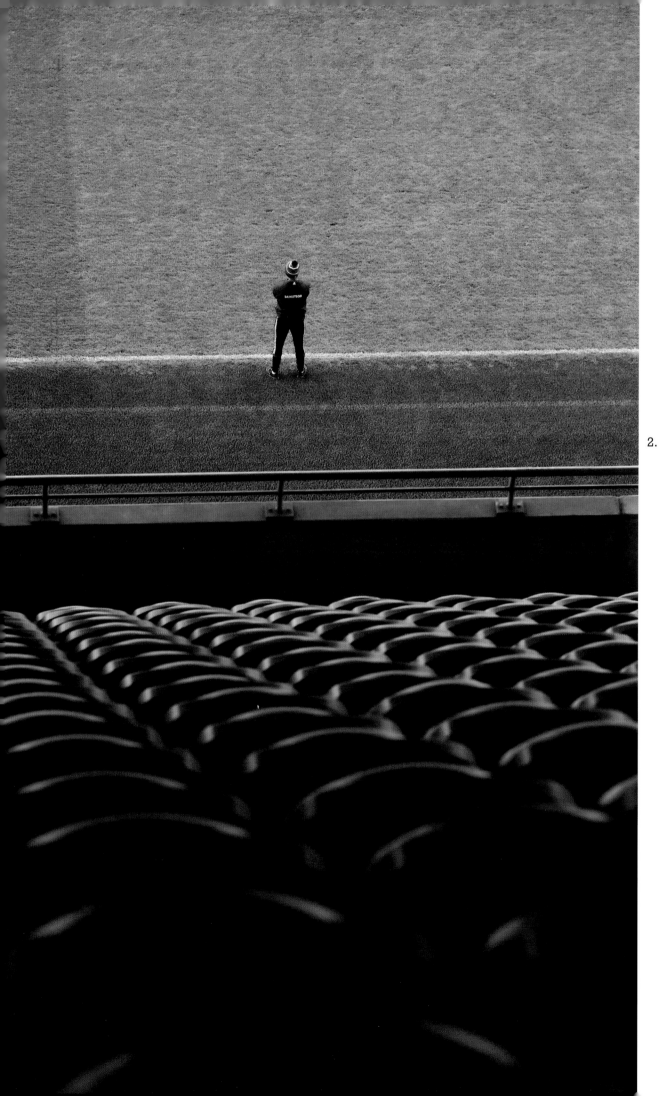

(1) The chosen few. Two stewards follow proceedings socially-distanced in an empty stand in Wexford Park as Séamus Casey launches a puck-out

(2-3) The sideline can be a lonely spot at the best of times. Waterford manager Liam Cahill surveys matters during his side's defeat in Páirc Uí Chaoimh – the only consolation is that he doesn't have to watch his back – while the face covering can't mask Meath manager Nick Weir's disappointment after a heavy defeat on home turf

15 Allianz Football League - Austin Stack Park, Tralee
Kerry 4-21   Galway 0-11

Allianz Football League - Geraldines Club, Haggardstown, Co Louth
Louth 3-08   Antrim 1-15

Allianz Football League - O'Neill's Healy Park, Omagh
Tyrone 0-16   Donegal 0-18

1.

2.

(1) Enter the footballers stage left. The second weekend of the season sees the start of the football league and it turns out to be a chastening experience for Galway in Tralee, beaten by 22 points. It's a case of history repeating itself given that they suffered a similar battering against Mayo in their first outing after lockdown the previous year

(2-3) Tapping into the Tyrone Blueprint. Mickey Harte makes his way to the dressing-room in Haggardstown for his first game as Louth manager and he won't have any difficulty recognising his counterparts in the Antrim dugout, manager Enda McGinley and selector Stephen O'Neill, two players he got to know well during his 18-year stint at the helm in Tyrone. Meanwhile, Harte's successors in the Red Hands hot seat, Feargal Logan and Brian Dooher, emerge at Healy Park

3.

15 Allianz Football League - Semple Stadium, Thurles
Cork 0-14   Kildare 2-12

Littlewoods Ireland Camogie League - Drom and Inch Club, Co Tipperary
Tipperary 0-14   Cork 2-13

1.

2.

(1) Home truths. Cork have to travel to Thurles to play Kildare having forfeited home advantage over a breach of the GAA's ban on team training during the Level 5 lockdown in January, and the result is costly. Here, Paul Walsh battles with Kildare midfielder Kevin Feely under the high ball

(2) Always keep your eye on the ball. Jill Ann Quirke of Tipperary and Cork's Kate Kilcommins stretch every sinew while maintaining their concentration in a full-blooded race for the sliotar

1.

15 Allianz Hurling League - MW Hire O'Moore Park, Portlaoise
Laois 1-19   Dublin 0-30

Allianz Hurling League - Semple Stadium, Thurles
Tipperary 0-22   Cork 2-16

2.

(1) Fist bumps de rigueur. It wasn't exactly a white-knuckle ride for Liam Rushe and his Dublin team-mate Fergal Whitley, here acknowledging their comfortable win against Laois the safe way

(2) Last man out, turn off the lights. Long after the Tipp and Cork hurlers have left centre stage, caretaker Andy Fox collects the sideline flags in a deserted Semple Stadium

" This is the sort of learning experience we need. Kilkenny knew how to close out the game and they did. But our players can be proud of their efforts **"**

Antrim manager Darren Gleeson after his young team's spirited effort against the Cats

1.

16 Allianz Football League - Dr Hyde Park, Roscommon
Roscommon 0-16   Dublin 1-22

Allianz Hurling League - UPMC Nowlan Park, Kilkenny
Kilkenny 1-28   Antrim 3-15

Allianz Hurling League - Walsh Park, Waterford
Waterford 1-22   Westmeath 1-19

2.

3.

(1) The unmistakable figure of Roscommon manager Anthony Cunningham, doing a passable impersonation of a second-hand car salesman, strides towards the pitch as Dublin come to town. There's no sales commission today however

(2) Poise, balance and no little speed. It's a bit of a blur as Eoghan Campbell chases down Eoin Cody in the Marble City where Antrim force Kilkenny to stay focused

(3) Close but no cigar. Westmeath are finding life extremely challenging in the first division although you take them for granted at your peril, as Waterford discover. However, even their best performance just comes up short and Aaron Craig shows his frustration at the final whistle

16   Allianz Football League - Brewster Park, Enniskillen
Monaghan 1-12   Armagh 1-16

Allianz Football League - Páirc Tailteann, Navan
Meath 0-16   Westmeath 0-15

Allianz Hurling League - Pearse Stadium, Salthill
Galway 0-26   Limerick 1-17

1.

2.

(1) A sprinkling of Star dust. While some counties are drawing on Tyrone know-how, Armagh look to the Kingdom and add Kieran Donaghy, a man with four All-Ireland senior medals and three All-Star awards, to their backroom team. Perhaps it's the Midas touch Armagh need at neutral Enniskillen, with Monaghan another team to lose home advantage for a Covid indiscretion

(2) Like Matthew Costello and Ethan Devine's aerial battle with Westmeath duo Sam Duncan and James Dolan, this game was up in the air until the very end when Meath came with a late surge to earn their first league win since March 2019

(3) By any means possible. The real fans support their team irrespective of whether they gain access to the grounds. Hammy Dawson, a clubmate of Gearóid Hegarty in St Patrick's, watches from outside Pearse Stadium while listening to the match on the radio

" It appears that the game of hurling has changed in the last four months. While we've all been at home, somebody decided to take the tackle out of the game **"**

Limerick manager John Kiely is not happy with the new advantage rule following his side's defeat to Galway

3.

22 Allianz Hurling League - Semple Stadium, Thurles
Tipperary 2-19   Galway 0-20

Allianz Football League - TEG Cusack Park, Mullingar
Westmeath 2-12   Mayo 0-21

(1) Happiness is. Goals are our business – that's the approach of Tipperary's lethal forwards and Noel McGrath has that special look of contentment after nailing his team's second against Galway

(2) Messi doesn't have to do this. With extra precautions required to combat Covid, some counties avoid travelling in team buses so Mayo's Jordan Flynn ends up buying his own parking ticket in Mullingar. The amateur ethos is preserved – it's not pay *for* play, it's pay *to* play

1.

2.

1.

(1) From the Europa League to the National League, from a full
house to an empty stadium. Laois goalkeeper Niall Corbet, who
got a taste of European soccer when he played with UCD in 2015,
is beaten all ends up by Cork forward Ruairí Deane's slick finish

(2) An eye to the main chance. With Niall McKenna of Antrim
for company, Dublin's Eoghan O'Donnell has his sights firmly
focused on the sliotar before making an overhead catch

2.

23 Allianz Football League - Semple Stadium, Thurles
Dublin 4-09 Kerry 1-18

Allianz Football League - Pearse Stadium, Salthill
Galway 2-16 Roscommon 1-13

1.

2.

(1) These heavyweights never fail to entertain. The Dublin and Kerry footballers shake and vacate at the end of another enthralling, high-scoring shoot-out that finishes level courtesy of David Clifford's last-minute penalty in Semple Stadium. Dublin are another team to forfeit home advantage because they breached the Covid training rules

(2) An attic conversion. The absence of supporters is still a precondition for hosting games so these fans in Salthill are putting their skylight to good use. Still, it's a tight squeeze in a two-up two-down

" We were poor last week against Kerry. It wasn't an acceptable performance and we trained hard during the week. None of the players who didn't start today were sulking and they were encouraging each other **"**

Galway manager Pádraic Joyce is heartened by the way his squad knuckled down following a heavy defeat in Tralee to beat Roscommon in Salthill

23

Allianz Football League - Athletic Grounds, Armagh
Down 0-14   Meath 2-15

Allianz Hurling League - MW Hire O'Moore Park, Portlaoise
Laois 1-17   Clare 2-27

Lidl Ladies National Football League - Parnell Park, Dublin
Dublin 6-15   Waterford 2-12

Allianz Hurling League - Walsh Park, Waterford
Waterford 1-22   Limerick 0-21

Lidl Ladies National Football League - MW Hire O'Moore Park, Portlaoise
Laois 2-16   Kildare 2-13

Allianz Hurling League - Páirc Uí Chaoimh, Cork
Cork 7-27   Westmeath 0-15

2.

1.

3.

4.

(1-2) The not so merry month of May. The unseasonal cold and wet weather sees Meath manager Andy McEntee drying his face with a bib and referee Patrick Murphy bracing himself for the start of the second half, accompanied by his linesmen Nicky O'Toole, left, and Nathan Wall

(3) Electric surge. One can feel the energy as Jodi Egan, one of the younger members of the Dublin panel, takes the game to Waterford's Kate McGrath

(4) A pressing engagement. Tom Morrissey demonstrates the effectiveness of Limerick's pressing game in forcing Waterford's Michael Kiely to rush his hand-pass

5.

6.

(5) This one's mine. Grace Clifford of Kildare takes command of the situation, pouncing on the ball ahead of Laois's Fiona Dooley

(6) A tough day at the office for Westmeath, whatever way you look at it. Cork are taking no prisoners this year as the Páirc Uí Chaoimh scoreboard confirms

29 Allianz Football League - Kingspan Breffni, Cavan
Cavan 2-11   Derry 1-16

Allianz Football League - Brewster Park, Enniskillen
Fermanagh 1-15   Longford 0-18

Allianz Football League - Athletic Grounds, Armagh
Armagh 1-16   Donegal 1-16

1.

2.

(1) Still going strong, and still delivering. Martin Reilly, playing his 152nd match for Cavan having made his debut in 2007, palms the ball to the Derry net despite the challenge of Michael McEvoy

(2) It starts with a trickle. Depending on where you live on the island, small numbers of supporters are once again permitted to attend games, although it's difficult to gauge what these spectators basking in the Enniskillen bleachers think about the return

(3) The one that got away. Armagh's Rory Grugan reacts to his team's home draw with Donegal, a game they let slip in the closing minutes

3.

30   Allianz Hurling League - UPMC Nowlan Park, Kilkenny
Kilkenny 2-27   Wexford 0-23

Allianz Football League - MW Hire O'Moore Park, Portlaoise
Laois 1-08   Kildare 2-18

1.

2.

(1) All togged out – apart from the boots – and somewhere to go. Conor Fogarty, right, leads his Kilkenny team-mates Conor Browne, Pádraig Walsh, TJ Reid and Huw Lawlor along O'Loughlin Road en route to Nowlan Park

(2) Fresh as a daisy. Laois goalkeepers Matthew Byron, left, and Niall Corbet, warm up on the training pitch in O'Moore Park before their clash with Kildare

30   Allianz Football League - Dr Hyde Park, Roscommon
Roscommon 1-12   Kerry 2-15

Allianz Football League - St Jarlath's Park, Tuam
Galway 1-15   Dublin 2-16

1.

(1) A bird's eye view. Roscommon players navigate the car park at Dr Hyde Park for the second half of their joust with Kerry under a watchful eye

(2) Forward march, eyes left. Putting their best foot forward, Ciarán Kilkenny, left, and Brian Fenton – two giants of the game – arrive in St Jarlath's Park

30 Allianz Football League - Elverys MacHale Park, Castlebar
Mayo 3-17 Meath 2-12

1.

2.

(1) Getting the names right. Last-minute team changes are the bane of a stadium announcer's life so John Hopkins double-checks his notes before Mayo host Meath in MacHale Park

(2) A place called home. Antrim supporters – among them Gerry Adams, the former president of Sinn Féin – flock to the recently upgraded facilities at Corrigan Park to see their team continue a promising league campaign with a draw against Wexford. Few counties have suffered more owing to the impasse around the redevelopment of Casement Park, which finally got the go-ahead for a 34,500-capacity stadium in July

(3) 23 on his back and 20 on the board. Described as the man with the adhesive touch, Clare's Tony Kelly continues to showcase his outrageous talents with a personal haul of 20 points against Dublin

5   Allianz Hurling League - Corrigan Park, Belfast
Antrim 1-21   Wexford 2-18

Allianz Hurling League - Parnell Park, Dublin
Dublin 2-23   Clare 0-34

3.

5 Allianz Hurling League - LIT Gaelic Grounds, Limerick
Limerick 0-33   Cork 2-19

6 Allianz Hurling League - UPMC Nowlan Park, Kilkenny
Kilkenny 1-29   Laois 0-22

1.

(1) Limerick v Cork – Part 1. A foreboding sky looms over the Mackey Stand as Pat Ryan bends to scoop the sliotar into his hand watched by Cork's Seán O'Leary. Limerick hold the aces in this, the first of three encounters between these sides before season's end

(2) A strong bench, a relaxed bunch. Kilkenny certainly have plenty of options if things go wrong against Laois with players like, from left, Niall Brassil, Darren Mullen, Richie Leahy, Cillian Buckley, TJ Reid, Conor Delaney and Walter Walsh waiting in the wings

❝ Was is a terrific display? No it wasn't, but we are walking away happy enough. Obviously we wanted to win and we have, and we got a good bit of game-time into a lot of the players on the panel **❞**

Kilkenny manager Brian Cody is as pragmatic as ever following his side's win over Laois, a victory that ensured the Cats finished top of Division 1B

6   Allianz Hurling League - TEG Cusack Park, Mullingar
Westmeath 0-16   Tipperary 4-27

Allianz Hurling League - Louth Centre of Excellence, Darver
Louth 3-16   Fermanagh 0-15

1.

2.

(1) A welcoming committee of one. Ten-year-old Evan Connolly – a Tipperary supporter
from Mullingar, a very select group – awaits the arrival of his team outside Cusack Park

(2) First trophy. GAA president Larry McCarthy speaks after the Division 3B match at
the Louth Centre of Excellence in Darver. His first trophy presentation as president is
to Louth hurling captain Feidhelm Joyce after the victory over Fermanagh

6 Allianz Hurling League - Pearse Stadium, Salthill
Galway 4-28 Waterford 3-23

Allianz Hurling League - Bord na Móna O'Connor Park, Tullamore
Offaly 5-25 Down 1-19

(1) There's no show like a Joe show. For all the artistry he brought to the game, Joe Canning wasn't afraid of the less glamorous stuff and here he pursues Séamus Keating and reaches to nick the ball from the Waterford man

(2) Sit down and make yourself at home. Brendan Monaghan from Kilcormac looks fairly chilled on his perch in O'Connor Park where he sees the Offaly hurlers conclude their promotion push to the top division

1.

2.

12 Allianz Football League - Páirc Tailteann, Navan
Wicklow 3-11   Cavan 0-18

Allianz Football League - Kingspan Breffni, Cavan
Dublin 1-18   Donegal 1-14

Allianz Hurling League - Cusack Park, Ennis
Clare 4-20   Kilkenny 1-25

Allianz Football League - Fitzgerald Stadium, Killarney
Kerry 6-15   Tyrone 1-14

1.

2.

3.

4.

(1) Wicklow goalkeeper Mark Jackson shows what it means to avoid the trapdoor to Division Four. Meanwhile, Cavan are in freefall, going from the top flight to the basement in three years

(2) A hands-on approach. Dublin midfielder Brian Fenton winces when a stray Donegal hand comes dangerously close to his eye

(3) In a tight corner. Clare defender Rory Hayes tries to avoid being boxed in by the Kilkenny trio of, from left, Eoin Cody, Alan Murphy and TJ Reid

(4) It's not often Tyrone are hit for six but Kerry forwards Tommy Walsh, left, and David Clifford seem quite matter of-fact after completing their latest demolition job in Killarney. The stakes will be much higher when these two meet in the championship

13 Allianz Football League - Athletic Grounds, Armagh
Armagh 1-17   Roscommon 0-11

Allianz Football League - Cusack Park, Ennis
Clare 2-18   Mayo 2-22

5.

6.

(5-6) We have your back. An Armagh supporter troops towards the Athletic Grounds while stewards in Ennis take up their positions on the covered terrace at Cusack Park. Victories enable Armagh to preserve their Division One status and Mayo to join them in the top tier

2.

(1) Light on their toes. On a perfect day for hurling, Ciarán Kirwan of Waterford avoids the long reach of Tipperary's Craig Morgan and claims possession in a battle between two of the younger members of the squads

(2) Join the club. Westmeath goalkeeper Noel Conaty and his defenders can't hide their disappointment after conceding a second goal against Limerick but they're not the first team – nor won't be the last – to have their spirit drained by the All-Ireland champions, to be literally brought to their knees

13

Littlewoods Ireland Camogie League - UPMC Nowlan Park, Kilkenny
Galway 1-19   Cork 1-17

Allianz Football League - St Conleth's Park, Newbridge
Kildare 1-14   Meath 0-14

Allianz Hurling League - Páirc Uí Chaoimh, Cork
Cork 2-23   Galway 3-25

Allianz Football League - St Tiernach's Park, Clones
Monaghan 1-21   Galway 2-17

1.

2.

3.

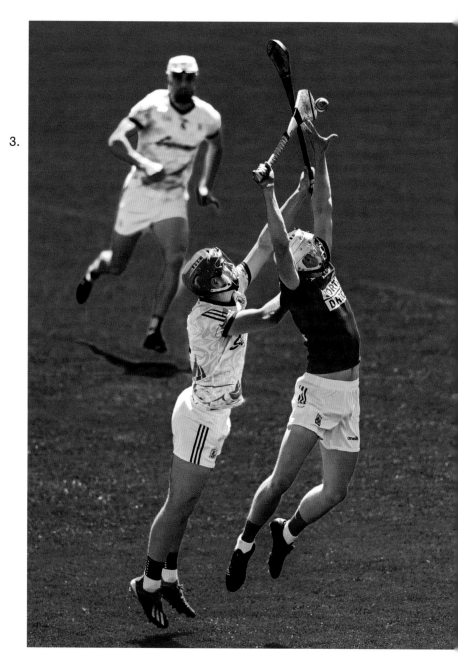

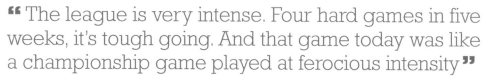

❝ The league is very intense. Four hard games in five weeks, it's tough going. And that game today was like a championship game played at ferocious intensity ❞

A very pleased Kildare manager Jack O'Connor following his side's win over Meath

4.

(1) Hanging in there. Cork captain Linda Collins strives might and main to halt a charge out of defence by one of Galway's most experienced players, Sarah Dervan

(2) Going up in the world. It's all smiles from Kildare manager Jack O'Connor and Brian McLoughlin after they hold off a Meath resurgence and clinch promotion to Division One

(3) Catch and protect. This is textbook overhead play from Cork corner forward Shane Barrett as he makes the catch and protects his hand ahead of Galway's TJ Brennan

(4) A debriefing session. Joint Monaghan stand-in managers Vinny Corey, left, and David McCague, kneeling, address the players in the company of their suspended manager Séamus McEnaney, who was present as a spectator. The theme of the talk could be the great escape as they claim a one-point extra-time victory to avoid the drop and instead consign Galway to Division Two

2.

❝ I just asked the girls to up the work rate. Aoife Doyle got a brilliant goal and that really drove us on for the second half ❞

**Kilkenny camogie manager Brian Dowling
on his half-time pep talk**

(1) The beginning of the end? A return to normality? A reopened Croke Park with around 2,400 spectators, who are allowed into the stadium as part of a Government test event, is a welcome sight after a year's absence. Certainly it's a welcome sight for Derry who hold too many aces for Offaly in the Division Three football final – the only league final played this year

(2) Crouch and swoop – two ambitious players going low but aiming high. Michelle Teehan knows from experience that a place on the Kilkenny team is hard earned and she's not going to make it easy for Galway forward Siobhán McGrath

26 Joe McDonagh Cup - Austin Stack Park, Tralee
Kerry 2-24   Down 1-21

Munster GAA Football Senior Championship - LIT Gaelic Grounds, Limerick
Limerick 4-18   Waterford 0-12

Connacht GAA Football Senior Championship - Markievicz Park, Sligo
Sligo 0-12   Mayo 3-23

Munster GAA Football Senior Championship - Fitzgerald Stadium, Killarney
Kerry 3-22   Clare 1-11

Leinster GAA Hurling Senior Championship - Páirc Tailteann, Navan
Dublin 3-31   Antrim 0-22

1.

2.

3.

(1) Seconds out. Kevin Hannafin, the Kerry hurling physio and occasional cutman, applies vaseline to Brendan O'Leary's eyebrows before the county's clash with Down

(2) The championship is back. But it's far from the glamour and the bright lights for Waterford football boss Shane Ronayne who finds himself setting up his team's warm-up for the match against Limerick – a manager has to be a jack of all trades in some counties

(3) A season-ending injury for Cillian O'Connor but is it season-ending for Mayo? The all-time highest scorer in championship history, sidelined with an Achilles tendon injury sustained in the league outing against Clare, watches his side dismantle Sligo

(4) Up and running. On a day when his full skillset was on display, Seán O'Shea wheels away after drilling Kerry's first goal of the championship and putting down a marker for the year

(5) No banana skin here. Dublin corner back Paddy Smyth shakes off a tackle from Shane Elliott as the Dubs similarly make light of a potentially tricky assignment against Antrim, and build confidence for bigger challenges ahead

26 Leinster GAA Hurling Senior Championship - UPMC Nowlan Park, Kilkenny
Wexford 5-31   Laois 1-23

Lidl Ladies National Football League Division 1 Final - Croke Park, Dublin
Dublin 2-15   Cork 1-13

1.

2.

(1) Only quiet when eating. The Wexford hurlers and backroom members are a picture of concentration fuelling up in Kilkenny after defeating Laois. It's a scene that highlights the measures team managements and county boards must take in order to provide meals for players during a pandemic

(2) First things first – wash your hands. Evergreen Dublin captain Sinéad Aherne, who made her intercounty debut back in 2003, takes the necessary precautions before acquainting herself with the Division One league trophy

27 Leinster GAA Football Senior Championship - Páirc Tailteann, Navan
Offaly 3-19   Louth 0-19

Leinster GAA Football Senior Championship - County Grounds, Aughrim
Wicklow 0-14   Wexford 2-11

2.

(1) The Faithful's most famous fan. Few things fire Shane Lowry's passion more than Offaly GAA and the 2019 British Open golf champion certainly enjoys this Leinster championship victory – only the county's third against any opposition since 2007

(2) Savour these days when they happen – particularly when it's a first success in the province since 2014. Elated Wexford manager Shane Roche celebrates with Seán Nolan after overcoming Wicklow in Aughrim

27 Ulster GAA Football Senior Championship - Páirc Esler, Newry
Down 1-12   Donegal 2-25

Munster GAA Hurling Senior Championship - Semple Stadium, Thurles
Clare 1-22   Waterford 0-21

1.

(1) Poetry in motion. An airborne Conor O'Donnell gets out in front of Down's James Guinness to claim possession. The only cloud on a good day for Donegal is a recurrence of Michael Murphy's hamstring injury

(2) Almost perfect symmetry. The athleticism, the artistry, the majesty of the greatest field game in the world are illustrated in this study of Waterford's Austin Gleeson and Aidan McCarthy of Clare launching themselves into the air

27 Leinster GAA Football Senior Championship - Bord na Móna O'Connor Park, Tullamore
Longford 0-25 Carlow 2-13

2.

1.

3.

❝ People say to me Brian's time in Kilkenny is up and they need some fresh blood. That's a load of rubbish. If Kilkenny people are thinking that, they need to have another look at themselves. What Brian has done is incredible and he is building a new team again ❞

Wexford hurling manager Davy Fitzgerald pays tribute to his Kilkenny counterpart Brian Cody after losing to the Cats in an extra-time thriller

3 Leinster GAA Hurling Senior Championship - Croke Park, Dublin
Dublin 1-18 Galway 1-14

Leinster GAA Hurling Senior Championship - Croke Park, Dublin
Kilkenny 2-37 Wexford 2-29

Ulster GAA Football Senior Championship - St Tiernach's Park, Clones
Monaghan 1-21 Fermanagh 0-14

Munster GAA Hurling Senior Championship - Semple Stadium
Limerick 2-22 Cork 1-17

4.

5.

(1) Job done, move on. Longford manager Padraic Davis and defender Enda Macken aren't losing the run of themselves after a routine win over Carlow

(2) Not many saw this one coming. Dublin stage the first shock of the hurling year and reach their first Leinster final since 2014, puncturing Galway's All-Ireland ambitions in the process. Substitute Jake Malone is enjoying the moment

(3) Just the usual thriller-cum-classic between Kilkenny and Wexford. Kilkenny goalkeeper Eoin Murphy lets rip knowing that victory is in the bag after Walter Walsh bats the Cats' second goal to the net late in injury time, just minutes after Murphy himself had pulled off a great save

(4) Protecting possession. Monaghan's Stephen O'Hanlon keeps the ball well away from Stephen McGullion as he runs at the Fermanagh defence

(5) Limerick v Cork – Part 2. Midfielder Darragh O'Donovan gets the first of two Limerick goals in first-half added time to undo all Cork's good work up to then and send them down the qualifiers route

4 Ulster GAA Football Senior Championship - Athletic Grounds, Armagh
Armagh 4-15   Antrim 0-14

Connacht GAA Football Senior Championship - Dr Hyde Park, Roscommon
Roscommon 0-12   Galway 2-11

(1) Pride in the jersey. Antrim supporter Pat McKay from Belfast nails his colours
to the mast in Armagh before his team run aground against the hosts

(2) It's great to be back. Honest. Galway supporter Des Casey from Ballybane,
left, shelters from the deluge at Dr Hyde Park before the game. Global warming
will make us appreciate the covered stand

1.

2.

4

Leinster GAA Football Senior Championship - Páirc Tailteann, Navan
Meath 4-22   Longford 0-12

Leinster GAA Football Senior Championship - Bord na Móna O'Connor Park, Tullamore
Westmeath 3-20   Laois 1-10

Leinster GAA Football Senior Championship - MW Hire O'Moore Park, Portlaoise
Kildare 1-15   Offaly 0-13

Munster GAA Hurling Senior Championship - LIT Gaelic Grounds, Limerick
Tipperary 3-23   Clare 2-22

3.

1.

2.

(1-3) Settling scores in Leinster. Meath's Fionn Reilly attempts to slip through the gate between the Longford duo of Patrick Fox, left, and Enda Macken en route to a 22-point victory; Kevin Maguire, left, and Rónan O'Toole link up after Westmeath rout Laois by 16 points; and Offaly's Eoin Carroll – Carroll by name and sponsor – mulls over his team's five-point defeat to Kildare

(4) The penalty that launched a thousand lips. Referee James Owens has no doubts that it's a penalty, and that the foul merited sending a Clare player to the sin-bin, in applying the new advantage rule, a decision that provokes a barrage of debate, criticism and abuse

" Look, we got the break today. We got the penalty and no better man than Jason Forde to stand up and put it in the back of the net "

Tipperary manager Liam Sheedy is happy to accept the good fortune that went his team's way in their clash with Clare

1.

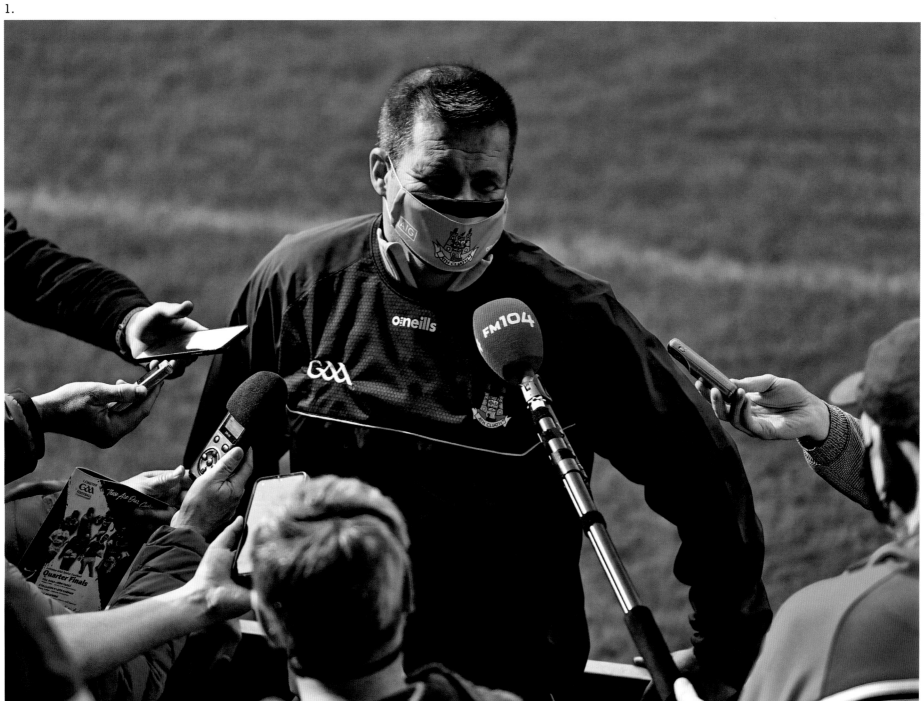

2.

(1) Hanging on his every word. Dublin manager Dessie Farrell participates in Question Time after being waylaid by the media but they're not inquiring about his health or his team's underwhelming start to the championship. Rather it's the whereabouts of Stephen Cluxton. All Dessie can say is that the man who likes to avoid the limelight has stepped away from the panel. A championship without Cluxton? Hamlet without the Prince

(2) How did it end up like this? Antrim's Eoghan Campbell is not hanging up his boots despite a demoralising defeat to Laois and a return to the Joe McDonagh Cup after only one season – one that started with such promise. In contrast, Laois, finding their best form, secure a place in the Liam MacCarthy Cup for next year

2.

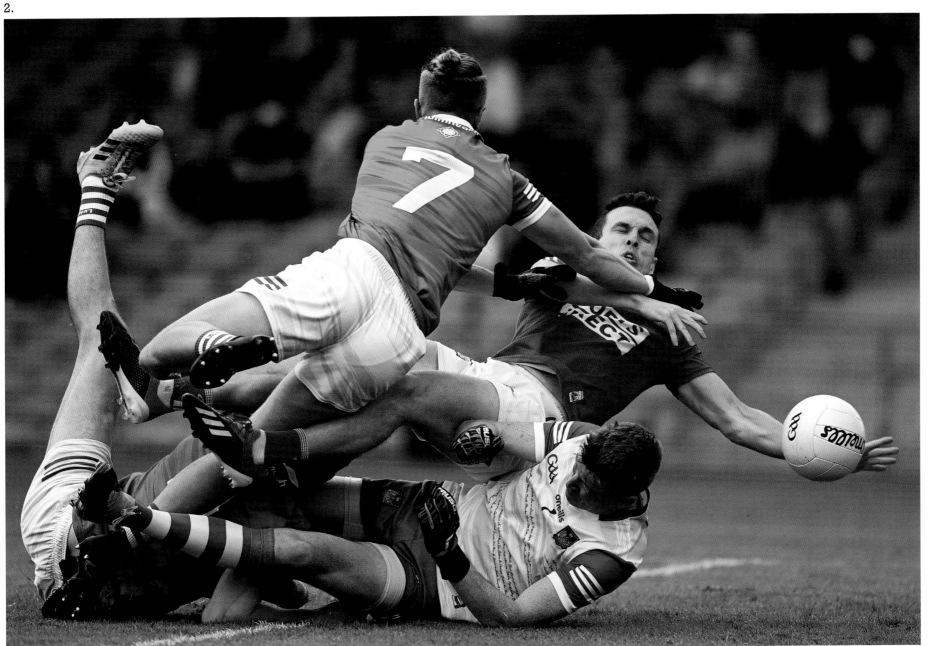

(1) Not according to plan. Going into the closing minutes, Cavan manager Mickey Graham knows the game is up. The highs of the 2020 Ulster title seem like a distant memory as relegation to the league basement is followed by a fall at the first championship hurdle

(2) Going in where it hurts. Amazingly, Cork's John O'Rourke lives to tell the tale after this old-fashioned goalmouth melee and he also manages – somehow – to stick the ball in the net. Limerick defenders Michael Donovan, left, and Gordon Brown also emerge unscathed but, unfortunately, goalkeeper Donal O'Sullivan wasn't so lucky and had to leave the field injured

10 Munster GAA Football Senior Championship - Semple Stadium, Thurles
Tipperary 1-08 Kerry 1-19

2020 Electric Ireland GAA Hurling All-Ireland Minor Championship Final - MW Hire O'Moore Park, Portlaoise
Galway 1-17 Kilkenny 1-14

(1) Two Evan Comerfords, there's only two Evan Comerfords. They represent Tipperary and Dublin and, by a coincidence, both are goalkeepers. The Tipp Evan Comerford looks shell-shocked after seeing the county's defence of the Munster title founder at the first fence – just like Cavan, the other surprise provincial champions of 2020

(2) Well worth the wait. After an 11-month delay and despite the lack of competitive action since their August 2019 All-Ireland win, Galway celebrate victory over Kilkenny in the 2020 minor hurling final, becoming the first team to win the Irish Press Cup four years in a row. From a Kilkenny perspective, it was the first time they lost three minor finals on the bounce

2.

1.

2.

(1) Rebel Rising. Conor O'Callaghan marks another important milestone in the resurgence of hurling in Cork, raising the James Nowlan Cup after they beat Dublin to claim the 2020 All-Ireland under-20 title

(2) Going right to the wire. Patrick McBrearty reacts after scoring a stunning winning point with 20 seconds of added time remaining to break Derry hearts in one of the best matches of the season. Ulster is the place for entertainment this summer

(3) A tough day at the office? RTÉ commentator Marty Morrissey, in the company of co-commentator Dessie Dolan, left, and statistician Dave Punch, struggles to generate some excitement with just a minute remaining and only a point for Leitrim to be added to the scoreboard

10 2020 Bord Gáis Energy GAA Hurling All-Ireland Under-20 Championship Final - UPMC Nowlan Park, Kilkenny
Cork 2-19   Dublin 1-18

11 Ulster GAA Football Senior Championship - MacCumhaill Park, Ballybofey
Donegal 0-16   Derry 0-15

Connacht GAA Football Senior Championship - Elverys MacHale Park, Castlebar
Mayo 5-20   Leitrim 0-11

3.

17 GAA Hurling All-Ireland Senior Championship Qualifiers Round 1 - UPMC Nowlan Park, Kilkenny
Waterford 3-23 Laois 2-21

GAA Hurling All-Ireland Senior Championship Qualifiers Round 1 - Semple Stadium, Thurles
Clare 2-25 Wexford 2-22

2.

(1) Cheddar and cream. With temperatures rising close to 30 degrees, it's a day for ice cream and taking it easy but Séamus Cheddar Plunkett resists the temptation from the nearby van, sticks with the dietary plan and continues his brisk walk to the dressing-rooms

(2) The Impartial Pundit. Arguably the most knowledgeable and entertaining hurling analyst around, Anthony Daly is first and foremost a loyal Clare man – memorably he captained the county to their breakthrough All-Ireland in 1995. So, the fist-pump is understandable when he sees the Banner's second goal against Wexford from the bowels of the Hogan Stand in Croke Park, where he is preparing to cover the Leinster final

2.

" Football will move on, but his family will never be the same again "

The tragic death the previous evening of Monaghan's under-20 captain, Brendan Óg Ó Dufaigh, is foremost in the mind of senior manager Séamus McEnaney ahead of their game with Armagh

(1-2) A day of heat and emotion – especially emotion. Some things are more important than sport and the tragic story behind this game – and all GAA events this weekend – was the death of Brendan Óg Ó Dufaigh, the captain of the Monaghan under-20 team who lost his life in a car crash the night before. Ó Dufaigh was described as a leader and a true gentleman. Pictured are an Armagh supporter making sensible use of his match programme during the heatwave and Monaghan's brilliant talisman Conor McManus celebrating at the final whistle having contributed 1-6 in an enthralling game of football

17 Joe McDonagh Cup Final - Croke Park, Dublin
Westmeath 2-28 Kerry 1-24

Leinster GAA Hurling Senior Championship Final - Croke Park, Dublin
Kilkenny 1-25 Dublin 0-19

1.

(1) Silverware and the Hogan Stand for a backdrop – not a bad day's work. After a challenging year in the league, Westmeath captain Cormac Boyle and his team-mates finally have something to shout about, a Joe McDonagh Cup triumph over Kerry who finish as runners-up for the second consecutive year

(2) Me and my shadow. Billy Ryan of Kilkenny, left arm outstretched, only has eyes for the ball as Dublin's Daire Gray gets up close and personal in the Leinster hurling final

2.

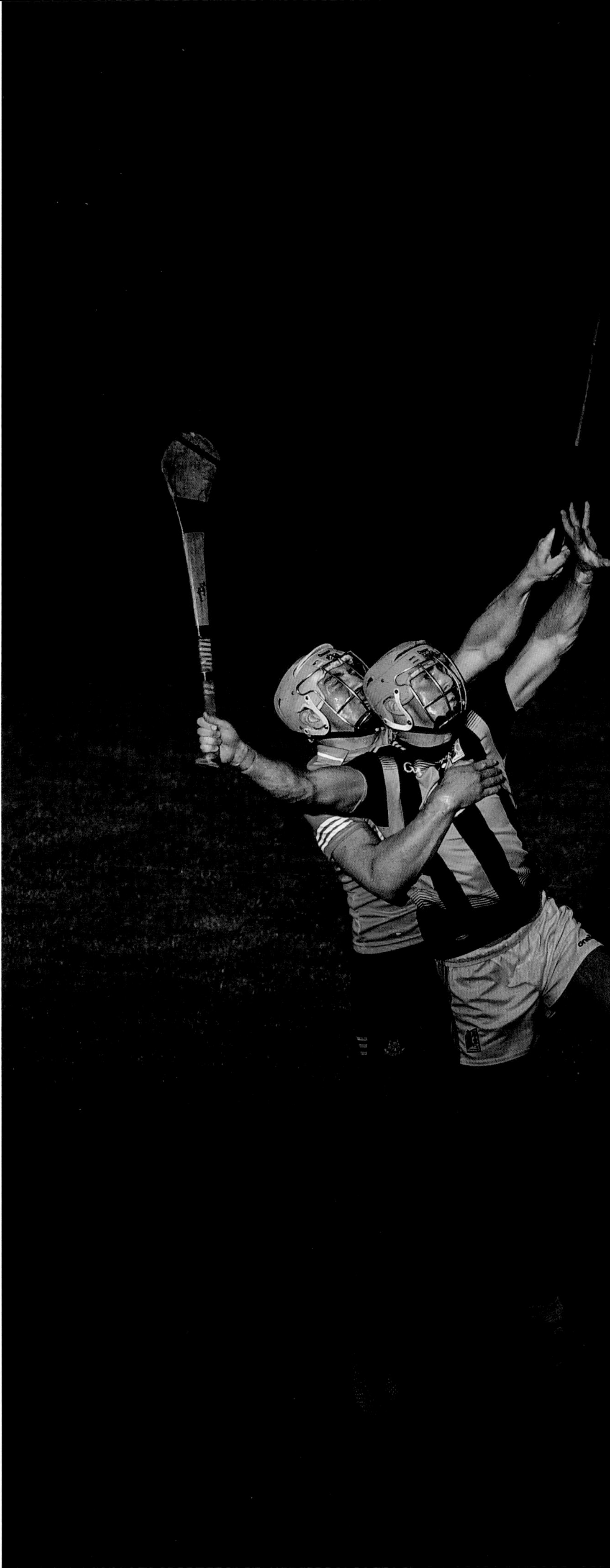

18 Leinster GAA Football Senior Championship - Croke Park, Dublin
Kildare 2-14 Westmeath 0-18

2020 Electric Ireland GAA Football All-Ireland Minor Championship Final
- Bord na Móna O'Connor Park, Tullamore
Derry 2-12 Kerry 1-14

Ulster GAA Football Senior Championship - Brewster Park, Enniskillen
Tyrone 0-23 Donegal 1-14

1.

2.

(1) Strong-arm tactics. Kildare's Daniel Flynn hangs on to the ball and Kevin Maguire hangs on to Flynn with the Lilywhites getting nothing easy from Westmeath – a place in the Leinster final is earned the hard way

(2) The Derry Heir. In captaining Derry to the 2020 All-Ireland minor football title, Matthew Downey is following a rich family legacy as his father Henry captained the county to their one and only success at senior level in 1993. Here, young Downey shows nerves of steel to convert a pressure penalty past Kerry goalkeeper Seán Broderick in the closing stages of the delayed final

(3) The second coming. Brilliant at minor level in 2012 and 2013 followed by a stint in Australian Rules with Essendon, Conor McKenna returned to Ireland and the GAA in September 2020 and is clearly relishing being back in the Tyrone family

3.

1.

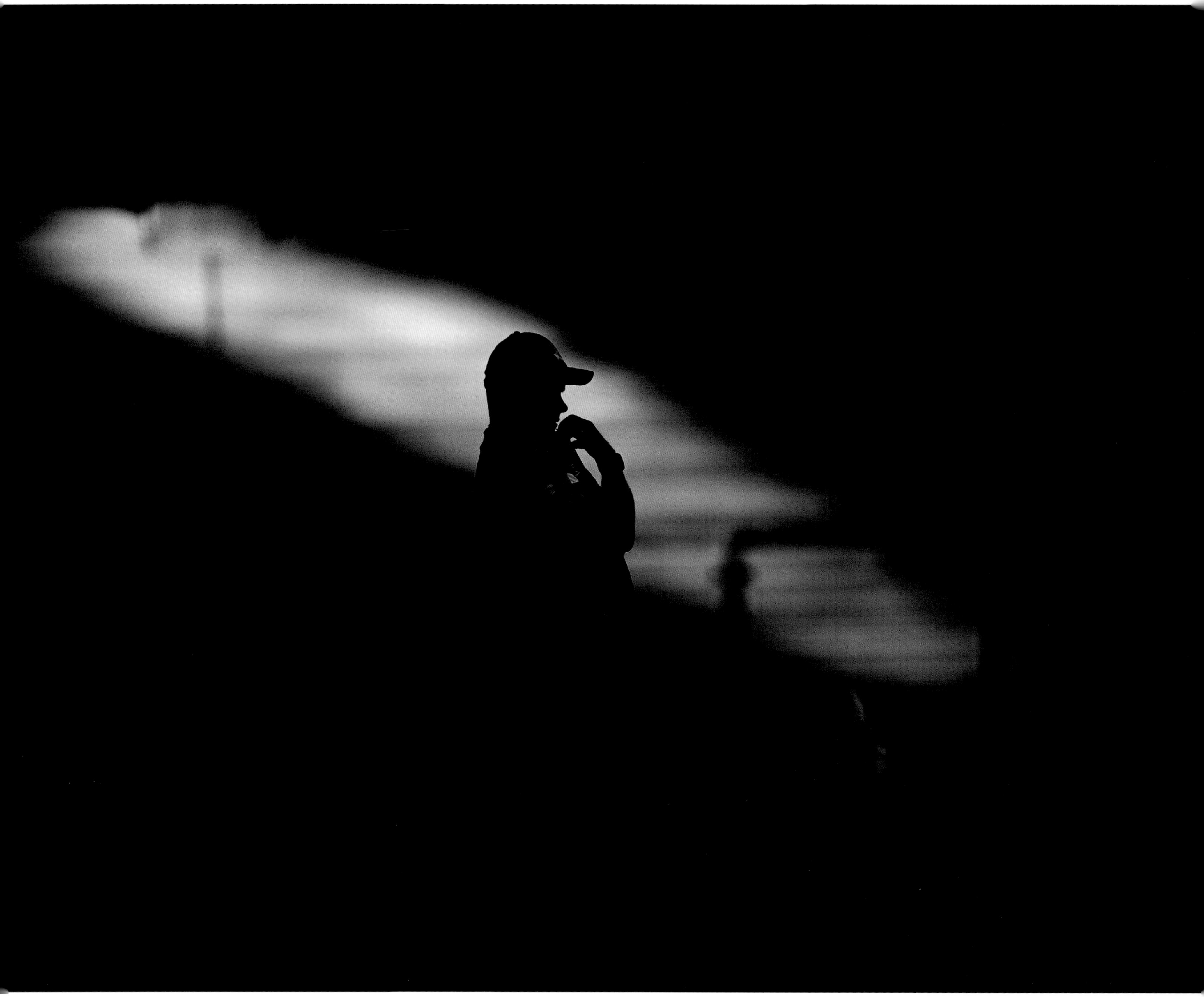

2.

" I'm extremely proud of the second-half performance, but the first half just wasn't good enough **"**

Meath manager Andy McEntee after his team gave Dublin a scare in their Leinster semi-final at Croke Park

(1) Watching from the shadows. The late afternoon light can play tricks in Croke Park and when Meath recovered from an 11-point half-time deficit Dublin manager Dessie Farrell must have wondered if he was seeing things. In the end, the champions steady the ship and stay on course for a seventh All-Ireland title in a row but there are small signs of vulnerability

(2) Goal of the year. Check. Comeback of the year. Check. Kyle Hayes salutes his memorable solo goal – running half the length of the pitch through the Tipperary defence – as Limerick overcome a 10-point half-time deficit to win another Munster title. Tipp duo Dan McCormack, left, and Cathal Barrett are helpless

24 GAA Hurling All-Ireland Senior Championship Qualifiers Round 2 - Semple Stadium, Thurles
Waterford 1-30   Galway 3-20

Allianz Hurling League Division 1 Relegation Play-off - MW Hire O'Moore Park, Portlaoise
Laois 1-27   Westmeath 0-27

1.

(1) The last act. Joe Canning troops off the field before informing his family and team-mates that this is his final game for the county. A once-in-a-generation player, he took his place in hurling history on the day, overtaking Henry Shefflin as the game's all-time record scorer in the championship with his haul of 27 goals and 485 points from 62 games. He also holds the record for sideline cuts with 28 in the championship. Ultimately, the wear and tear on his body was the decisive factor after 14 years of sheer class in the maroon jersey

(2) A spy on the wall. Even the extra layer of blocks on the O'Moore Park perimeter proves no deterrent for this Laois supporter keen to witness the hurlers' successful mission to stay in the top division of the league

❝ That's it, I'm finished with Galway. I told the boys in the dressing-room that was it, so I have to keep my word. I will keep playing with Portumna but that's me finished with Galway ❞

Joe Canning is very matter-of-fact in announcing his retirement from inter-county hurling

2.

(1) Ground hurling. Not many hurlers can strike the sliotar over the bar from a kneeling position but Patrick Horgan makes it look easy when scoring Cork's second point in a thrilling match – not a deflected score but a genuflected one

(2) End of the road. John Conlon, relocated to centre back this season with great success, tries to come to terms with a narrow defeat just as hope was building for the Banner

25 Connacht GAA Football Senior Championship Final - Croke Park, Dublin
Mayo 2-14   Galway 2-08

Munster GAA Football Senior Championship Final - Fitzgerald Stadium, Killarney
Kerry 4-22   Cork 1-09

1.

(1) Reflected glory. The Connacht final is relocated to Croke Park to accommodate a crowd of 18,000 and the switch suits Mayo just fine, as can be gleaned from a beaming Lee Keegan with his 14-month-old daughter Líle and the Nestor Cup. This is not the first time the Connacht decider moved west to east as the replayed 1922 final between Galway and Sligo took place on Jones' Road in September 1923

(2) According to plan. Kerry's plan, quite simply, was to ensure that last year's calamity against Cork was not repeated – no last-minute killer goals please. Scoring 4-22 against their old rivals was a bonus, so too was a two-goal haul for Paul Geaney while David Clifford's tally of just one point was a curiosity and not something that bothered him unduly judging by his warm reaction to Geaney's second goal

2.

" We had a good day and the scoreboard turned nicely for us. You go back to last year's semi-final and the scoreboard didn't turn for us. There is a great sense of unity in the squad and a great work ethic in the team "

Kerry manager Peter Keane is pleased there was no repeat of last year's shock defeat to Cork

28 Electric Ireland Leinster GAA Hurling Minor Championship Final - Netwatch Cullen Park, Carlow
Kilkenny 1-15   Wexford 2-10

Somewhere under the rainbow. Nature provides the perfect setting – a multi-coloured domed roof – in Carlow for one of Leinster's great rivalries. Kilkenny minor hurling captain Harry Shine and his opposite number, Wexford's Luke Murphy, wait to see how referee Thomas Gleeson's coin lands before choosing ends. No crock of gold for the winners but they'll settle for silverware

28 Munster GAA Hurling Under-20 Championship Final - Páirc Uí Chaoimh, Cork
Cork 1-26   Limerick 1-24

30 EirGrid Ulster GAA Football Under-20 Championship Final - Athletic Grounds, Armagh
Down 3-15   Monaghan 1-14

1.

(1) A well-kept secret? In terms of quality hurling, tight matches and the development of players, the Munster under-20 championship – previously the under-21 – is something of a hidden gem in the GAA's calendar. Aficionados check for the stars of tomorrow and Cork's Darragh Flynn, whose 12 points in the final helped beat Limerick to this year's title, may be one to watch out for

(2) "There's bigger things than football here." In these few words the player of the match, Down's Ruairi O'Hare, captured the feelings of many on another emotionally-charged evening for Monaghan. Two weeks after the death of their under-20 captain Brendan Óg Ó Dufaigh, Monaghan had to lift themselves to face Down in the final. It was a dignified occasion – the Monaghan players wore black armbands and the number six shirt, Ó Dufaigh's position, was left blank on the match-day programme

31 Ulster GAA Football Senior Championship Final - Croke Park, Dublin
Tyrone 0-16   Monaghan 0-15

(1-2) A novel fixture, but the same attention to detail. The Ulster final is added to the list of games moved to Croke Park to take advantage of the larger crowds permitted at headquarters. Here, groundsman Enda Colfer places a sideline flag after the stadium's white lines are touched up and, at the end of proceedings, Darren McCurry and his Tyrone team-mates are the ones bringing the Anglo-Celt Cup back north after a narrow win over Monaghan

1.

2.

" There is no tomorrow in football and that keeps you motivated, keeps you on the edge. We preach it to our guys and thankfully they stood up to a man. Tyrone has a deep-rooted tradition in Gaelic football, something that is not lost on Brian Dooher and myself in our management roles **"**

Tyrone joint manager Feargal Logan's first season in charge continues to get better

31 GAA Hurling All-Ireland Senior Championship Quarter-Final - Páirc Uí Chaoimh, Cork
Waterford 4-28 Tipperary 2-27

GAA Hurling All-Ireland Senior Championship Quarter-Final - Semple Stadium, Thurles
Cork 2-26 Dublin 0-24

1.

(1) Hurling or football? Austin Gleeson has lost his hurley but he carries on regardless and his right-foot kicked effort forces Tipperary goalkeeper Barry Hogan into a diving save. The Déise score a first championship win over their neighbours since 2008 and so bring an end to Liam Sheedy's second tenure in charge

(2) It's dropping. Dublin full back Paddy Smyth steals a few inches on Patrick Horgan but it's the end of the road for the men in blue after scuttling Galway's hopes in Leinster but another step in the right direction for the Rebels, with momentum and belief building

“ I know they wouldn't want pity, because that's not the type of players they are, but I do feel sorry that Tipperary are knocked out of the championship by a team that I manage ”

Waterford manager Liam Cahill, a former Tipperary star, reflects on his native county's exit from the championship

31 Lory Meagher Cup Final - Croke Park, Dublin
Fermanagh 3-26   Cavan 1-17

1.

2.

(1) Start at the bottom. The only way is up for teams in the Lory Meagher Cup, the fifth-tier competition for the weakest counties, but Fermanagh are savouring their success and enjoying the limelight associated with performing at headquarters

(2-3) Remember Offaly's hurlers? They were seriously handy one time. The Faithful have been playing off Broadway in recent years but their supporters haven't completely given up on them, particularly Seán Hassett, Ronan McNamara, Gearóid McCormack and Cian Burke, who applaud one of their 41 points in winning the Christy Ring Cup. Next year it's the Joe McDonagh, still a long way from the Liam MacCarthy, still a long way from their box-office days – manager Michael Fennelly, on the right, has more work to do

1 Christy Ring Cup Final - Croke Park, Dublin
Offaly 0-41   Derry 2-14

3.

1

TG4 All-Ireland Ladies Senior Football Championship Quarter-Final - St Tiernach's Park, Clones
Meath 3-15 Armagh 1-14

Leinster GAA Football Senior Championship Final - Croke Park, Dublin
Dublin 0-20 Kildare 1-09

Electric Ireland Leinster GAA Football Minor Championship Final - Bord na Móna O'Connor Park, Tullamore
Meath 3-08 Dublin 1-03

1.

2.

(1) Fast learners. Meath are making the transition from intermediate level to senior look easy and Niamh O'Sullivan and Aoibhín Cleary, number 6, are overjoyed after their shock victory over Armagh. The sentiment is decidedly different in the favourites' camp

(2) Hang time. Ciarán Kilkenny seems to be taking a giant leap in the dark as he jumps towards the dropping ball with Shea Ryan of Kildare for company. Not vintage Dublin on this afternoon but Kilkenny is his usual influential self as they make it 11 Leinster titles in a row. But most people have stopped counting

(3) If it's worth doing, it's worth doing twice. A little over a month after they won the 2020 Leinster title, the Meath minors lift the 2021 edition, taking the scalps of Offaly and Dublin in the finals. The winning feeling just gets better

3.

6 Electric Ireland Connacht GAA Football Minor Championship Final - Dr Hyde Park, Roscommon
Sligo 0-19   Roscommon 1-11

1.

(1-2) Devastation for one team, deliverance for the other. The long wait is over for Sligo with
the county winning their first Connacht minor title since 1968, a jubilant Kyle Davey
becoming only their third captain to raise the cup. Who would begrudge a success-starved
county like Sligo. For Roscommon's Conor Harley, left, and Rory Hester it's a tough one to
take after doing the donkey work in the province by beating Mayo and Galway

2.

7 GAA Hurling All-Ireland Senior Championship Semi-Final - Croke Park, Dublin
Limerick 1-25   Waterford 0-17

EirGrid GAA Football All-Ireland Under-20 Championship Semi-Final - Kingspan Breffni, Cavan
Roscommon 2-13   Down 1-10

2.

❝ From the get-go we had good shape and structure to what we were about. But I still think we have a bit more in us in that regard ❞

Limerick manager John Kiely reckons there is more in his team despite their 11-point win over Waterford

(1) Positional sense. One gets a great insight into players' movement on the pitch in this overhead shot, with Limerick's defenders drawn to the man in possession and the Waterford forwards fanning out to find space. But it all matters little with someone like Kyle Hayes around as he deftly dispossesses Patrick Curran and snuffs out the danger

(2) The Rossie Roar. No prizes for guessing who won this match, the clue being Jason Doory's no-holds-barred reaction at the final whistle. Roscommon will see victory as some consolation for the minors' defeat to Sligo and will be chuffed at putting one over a well-prepared Down outfit under manager Conor Laverty and the heavyweights in his backroom team – Meath legend Seán Boylan and former Australian Rules player Marty Clarke

1.

2.

3.

(1) Colour coded, Cody colours. The Hogan Stand's dressing-room number one is suitably painted for the arrival of the Kilkenny team and manager Brian Cody for a marathon clash with Cork. Now in his 23rd season at the helm, Cody is the longest serving manager in hurling and has equalled Seán Boylan's 23 seasons with the Meath footballers

(2) The masses are returning – 24,000 to be precise – and so is the atmosphere. The Davin Stand seats take on a distinctly red hue as socially-distanced supporters stand for Amhrán na bhFiann before the Cork-Kilkenny semi-final

(3) Opportunity knocks. Kilkenny supporter Michael Gannon, from the Marble City, takes a photograph outside the house of Irish Olympic gold medallist Kellie Harrington on Portland Row. Earlier that morning Kellie's exploits in the ring captured the hearts of the nation

8 GAA Hurling All-Ireland Senior Championship Semi-Final - Croke Park, Dublin
Cork 1-37   Kilkenny 1-32

4.

5.

(4) Surgical precision under pressure. Time is almost up, Kilkenny are three points behind and need a goal, the opposition have the ball, the Cats are in a hole and, well, no prizes for guessing what happens next. Pádraig Walsh dispossesses Tim O'Mahony, sends an inch-perfect pass to Adrian Mullen near the Cork goal and Mullen finds enough space to fire an equalising goal past goalkeeper Patrick Collins and bring the game to extra time. Ice in the veins. Pure Kilkenny

(5) Book the buses for the final. With a place in the All-Ireland senior final secured for the first time since 2013, this is justification for Kieran Kingston's emphasis on youth and pace. Time to celebrate with selector Diarmuid O'Sullivan, always a Rock of support

" That's why we have a bench. We expect the subs we bring on will impact the game for us "

Cork selector Diarmuid O'Sullivan on what the management expect from their squad

8 GAA Hurling All-Ireland Senior Championship Semi-Final -
Croke Park, Dublin
Cork 1-37   Kilkenny 1-32

Electric Ireland Munster GAA Football Minor Championship Final -
Semple Stadium, Thurles
Cork 1-17   Limerick 0-13

1.

(1) Never look back – the result is the result. His media interviews
over, the ever-obliging Brian Cody makes that lonely walk down
the tunnel to the Kilkenny dressing-room. However, he'll be back
for his 24th season in charge in 2022 – after all, Croke Park is
where he belongs

(2) Another band of Rebels rocking and rolling. The Cork conveyor
belt of talent is working efficiently in both codes, and this time it's
the turn of the county's minor footballers to whoop it up – especially
after breaking Kerry's eight-year stranglehold on the competition in
the semi-final and then accounting for Limerick in the final

2.

AUGUST '21

13 Electric Ireland Ulster GAA Football Minor Championship Final - Brewster Park, Enniskillen
Tyrone 2-11   Donegal 1-07

14 TG4 All-Ireland Ladies Senior Football Championship Semi-Final - Croke Park, Dublin
Dublin 1-17   Mayo 2-09

2.

(1) A meteoric rise. Just four and half months after being appointed manager, Gerard Donnelly guides the Tyrone minors to an Ulster title, the county's first since 2012. With former stars Conor Gormley and Ciaran Gourley in his backroom, it's a dream team – no wonder Donnelly is getting the bumps from his players

(2) Putting their game faces on. The Dublin ladies football team, aiming for a fifth senior title in a row, know the drill at this stage as they break away after the team photo. Former Ireland rugby international Hannah Tyrrell scores five points from play in this semi-final and is named player of the match, crowning a wonderful week in which she got married

2.

(1-2) It's the hope that kills you. Or keeps you going? Anthony Battle, left,
and Antel Zsabo, from Ballina, arrive in Croke Park to join the eternal
optimists from the west and the serious pragmatist – in situ early – from the
east. There is a sense of something momentous about to happen between
the team that doesn't know how to lose the big matches and the team that
doesn't know how to win them. Or so it seems

14   GAA Football All-Ireland Senior Championship Semi-Final - Croke Park, Dublin
      Mayo 0-17   Dublin 0-14

1.

2.

(1) Calm and calming. James Horan's composure and quiet demeanour on the sideline, even when things are not going well, is a constant, and a constant reassurance to the Mayo players. His mantra is don't panic, there's always time, there's always a next time

(2-3) How would this register on the Richter Scale? This is the day the empire crumbled with Mayo ending Dublin's 45-match unbeaten reign in the championship. It's into the trenches from the word go in this titanic match with Mayo's Diarmuid O'Connor and James Ruane jostling for possession with Brian Fenton and James McCarthy from Dublin at the throw-in, and it's equally touch tight in this contest between Fenton and Paddy Small and Ruane and Michael Plunkett

3.

" We were probably tentative about whether we should push forward or hold back a little bit in the first 15-20 minutes. We got caught in that maybe. But we managed to lift the energy for the second half and things took off from there **"**

How Mayo manager James Horan saw his county's first championship win over the Dubs in nine attempts

14 GAA Football All-Ireland Senior Championship Semi-Final - Croke Park, Dublin
Mayo 0-17   Dublin 0-14

1.

2.

(1-2) A match-defining moment. Diarmuid O'Connor seems to be chasing a lost cause when
he races along the endline and, at full stretch, gets a boot to a Rob Hennelly free that is going
wide. He manages to keep the ball in play for Kevin McLoughlin to collect and swing over the
bar, and over an attempted blockdown by John Small. In a game of inches and small margins,
it's a point made by Mayo – literally and figuratively

(3) Take Two. Mayo goalkeeper Rob Hennelly – under all sorts of pressure having kicked
a 45 for an equaliser well wide seven minutes into injury time – shows his mental toughness
when dramatically given a second chance and so brings the game to extra time.
Redemption for Hennelly after a nightmare in the 2016 replay

3.

❝ We were very flat in the second half. We knew that Mayo, similar to what they did in the Connacht final, were going to come with a lot. I think we found it very difficult to get out past their high press and we struggled to build any sort of momentum ❞

Dublin manager Dessie Farrell tries to analyse the All-Ireland champions' second-half slump

14 GAA Football All-Ireland Senior Championship Semi-Final - Croke Park, Dublin
Mayo 0-17 Dublin 0-14

(1) Coming of age. The dash and panache of Tommy Conroy, here celebrating after kicking a mighty point in extra time, were crucial in Mayo's win over the greatest team of all time. In winning a record six All-Ireland titles in a row, Dublin set new standards in the game but this is the year some of the chasing pack caught up

(2) Coming out of obscurity. Pádraig O'Hora goes from being a squad player to man of the match in the space of a few months. Afterwards he finds the words that best sum up Mayo: "We always seem to put ourselves at the bottom of the hill before we go climbing it." No better way to mark the occasion than a hug with his children Caiden and Mila-Rae – and the cuddly toy

1.

2.

1.

2.

3.

4.

" There won't be a golf ball
hit in Offaly for a week **"**

Twitter reaction to Shane Lowry's presence
at the All-Ireland under-20 football final

5.

6.

O Come On Ye Faithful. 2021 may yet be remembered as the year Offaly as a county turned a corner after decades in the doldrums in both codes and at all levels. In this sequence from their under-20 final success (1) Jack Bryant rifles the ball to the Roscommon net in the 50th minute and (2) celebrates with midfielder Morgan Tynan; (3) Aaron Brazil joins the Offaly supporters who descended on the capital in huge numbers having taken this team to their hearts; (4) those supporters include golfer Shane Lowry whose father Brendan won an All-Ireland senior medal in 1982; (5) captain Kieran Dolan, brought on as a substitute by Offaly manager Declan Kelly, lifts the Clarke Cup; and finally (6) it's time for the whole squad and backroom team to let their hair down

15 TG4 All-Ireland Ladies Senior Football Championship Semi-Final - Croke Park, Dublin
Meath 2-12   Cork 2-10

2.

(1-2) Remember the name. Emma Duggan, the 19-year-old who sat her Leaving
Cert this summer and scored 1-5 in this semi-final, shoots low to the net with 30
seconds of normal time remaining – Meath's second goal in the final minute –
to complete a great comeback. It also completes the Royals' remarkable
transformation from the dark days of the 2015 All-Ireland qualifiers when they
lost by 40 points to Cork. No wonder they're celebrating wildly

18 GAA Hurling All-Ireland Under-20 Championship Final - Semple Stadium, Thurles
Cork 4-19   Galway 2-14

21 Electric Ireland GAA Hurling All-Ireland Minor Championship Final - Semple Stadium, Thurles
Cork 1-23   Galway 0-12

2.

(1-2) There's something stirring down south. Cork claim under-20 and minor All-Ireland hurling crowns in a three-day period in the run-up to the senior final, and Galway feel the pain on both occasions. The minors were particularly impressive in ending the county's 20-year wait for an All-Ireland title at this grade, winning their four matches by an average margin of 19 points. Now the pressure is on the Cork seniors to complete a Rebel Treble

2.

(1) Limerick v Cork – Part 3. Pods if you please. Empty seats are a rare sight on All-Ireland final day but Covid crowd restrictions mean only 40,000 are permitted to attend the third meeting of Cork and Limerick this season, the one that matters most

(2) The Limerick masterclass starts on time. Gearóid Hegarty, the big man for the big occasion, strikes his team's first goal after just two minutes. The onslaught that follows sends shock and awe through the game and Cork, for all the progress made this year, can do little about it. As their manager Kieran Kingston remarked afterwards: "It was like trying to stop the tide with a bucket"

22 GAA Hurling All-Ireland Senior Championship Final - Croke Park, Dublin
Limerick 3-32   Cork 1-22

(1) Top corner, top drawer. Cork respond with a goal of their own in the exhilarating opening exchanges thanks to Shane Kingston, justifying his father's decision to start him after he contributed seven points as a substitute in the semi-final. The Cummins logo on the sliotar is visible as Nickie Quaid and Dan Morrissey follow its flight

(2) Stay in your lane, play between the lines. It's a case of pitch perfect as the players from two proud counties work their way into the contest, like miniature figures moving on a table. Subbuteo hurling

1.

2.

22 GAA Hurling All-Ireland Senior Championship Final - Croke Park, Dublin
Limerick 3-32   Cork 1-22

All over bar the shouting. Gearóid Hegarty and Limerick's passionate supporters are already in celebratory mode after the 2020 Hurler of the Year had scored his second goal and the team's third in the 35th minute. It's sensational stuff. The Treaty's half-time tally of 3-18 would have been enough to win 109 of the previous All-Ireland finals, and even halfway through the game the question being posed by many is – have we seen a better team?

" We got things right from the start today in terms of our set-up. We got our energy levels right, started putting a lot of pressure on Cork ball coming out of defence and, most of all, when we had the ball ourselves we used it really well and managed to create a lot of space up front. Our accuracy also was very good **"**

John Kiely sums up what was a perfect day in the office for his Limerick team

22   GAA Hurling All-Ireland Senior Championship Final - Croke Park, Dublin
Limerick 3-32   Cork 1-22

1.

(1) **By leaps and bounds.** Barry Nash shows exquisite judgement and timing to hold off Shane Kingston in this aerial battle. On the day, Limerick had 13 different scorers and one of the biggest cheers was reserved for the corner back when he came forward to strike over a fine point

(2) **Giants' Stadium.** By combining their height, physique and power with their skill and work rate, Limerick have raised standards to a higher level – literally and metaphorically. Cork's Robbie O'Flynn has little hope with the imposing figures of Kyle Hayes and Gearóid Hegarty, both 6ft 5ins tall, blocking him over and under. It's a microcosm of the work ethic that underpins what is fast becoming a team for the ages

❝ It was like trying to stop the tide with a bucket. No matter what we tried – go short or go long – they were just at another level to Cork today. We have got to be honest and say that **❞**

Cork manager Kieran Kingston pays tribute to Limerick's power

1.

2.

(1) A tour de force. Cian Lynch catches the ball in his right hand ahead of Mark Coleman in a near perfect performance from the Limerick playmaker-cum-magician, which prompted RTÉ pundit and former Cork goalkeeper Donal Óg Cusack to remark: "Playing against Cian Lynch is like trying to play hurling against Harry Potter"

(2) Getting used to this. For the third time in four seasons Limerick captain Declan Hannon does the honours on behalf of Team Green, lifting the Liam MacCarthy Cup in triumph. The Adare player becomes the fourth man to captain three All-Ireland senior hurling successes, following in the footsteps of Tipperary's Mikey Maher, Kilkenny's Dick 'Droog' Walsh and Cork's Christy Ring. And Limerick's score of 3-32 is a record total for an All-Ireland final, eclipsing Kilkenny's 3-30 in 2008 and Tipperary's 2-29 in 2016

(3) Mastermind. Manager John Kiely normally remains pensive while patrolling the sideline during a match but he's as entitled as anyone to embrace the celebrations in front of Hill 16 with the Liam MacCarthy Cup

(4) They couldn't be in safer hands. Limerick goalkeepers Nickie Quaid and Barry Hennessy introduce a future generation to Croke Park – Nickie's six-month-old son Daithí and Barry's four-week-old daughter Hope

4.

The Limerick family. No All-Ireland winning squad returns with the exact same personnel the following year so this snapshot in time will never be repeated. Whether Limerick can be stopped any time soon is another proposition. And, keeping it in the family, five of Limerick's starting 15 have fathers who represented the county with distinction – Nickie Quaid, Barry Nash, Gearóid Hegarty, Séamus Flanagan and Seán Finn whose fathers are Tommy Quaid, Mike Nash, Ger Hegarty, John Flanagan and Brian Finn

28 Electric Ireland GAA Football All-Ireland Minor Championship Final - Croke Park, Dublin
Meath 1-12   Tyrone 1-11

1.

2.

(1) Put it up. Oisín Ó Murchú wheels away after scoring Meath's crucial goal against Tyrone in the All-Ireland minor football final. Ó Murchú was the Royals' top scorer with 1-2 but it was Shaun Leonard – keeping his nerve – who kicked the winning point in the 64th minute for the back-to-back Leinster champions

(2) Full back, captain and man of the match, it's a day to remember for a clearly elated Liam Kelly as the Meath player lifts the Tom Markham Cup

(3) Happy faces all. The victorious Meath panel and backroom team members rejoice after winning their first All-Ireland minor title since 1992. Success is always sweeter against powerful opponents and Tyrone, who cruised through the Ulster championship with 53 points to spare and hammered Cork by 14 in the semi-final, were formidable

3.

28 GAA Football All-Ireland Senior Championship Semi-Final - Croke Park, Dublin
Tyrone 3-14   Kerry 0-22

2.

1.

3.

(1-2) They've arrived – and to prove it they're here. The Red Hand army, with Niall Morgan leading the way, finally reach the Croke Park dressing-rooms and then make their way on to the pitch, but it was touch and go for a while. A Covid outbreak in the camp seriously disrupted Tyrone's preparations and they informed GAA authorities that they would not be in a position to field a team on the original date for this semi-final. But Kerry and the GAA agreed to an extension, a sporting gesture that ensured the integrity of the competition

(3) And so begins the game that might never have been. And the shock that might never have happened. Referee David Coldrick throws in the ball between Kerry's David Walsh and Jack Barry and Tyrone's rookie midfield pairing of Conn Kilpatrick and Brian Kennedy

(4-5) Goals win games – Exhibit A. While the high-scoring Kerry attack fails to find the back of the net, Tyrone's clinical finishing wins the day with Niall McKenna slotting home their first goal and substitute Cathal McShane pouncing for their second. And there's an Aussie Rules connection with both goals as McKenna played for Essendon in Australia and McShane was on the verge of going Down Under in January 2020 before a last-minute change of mind

28 GAA Football All-Ireland Senior Championship Semi-Final - Croke Park, Dublin
Tyrone 3-14 Kerry 0-22

1.

2. 3.

(1-2) What a difference, and what a turnaround. Kieran McGeary and Paudie Clifford must be scratching their heads when they think back to the league match on June 12th when Kerry stuck six goals in the Tyrone net. Clifford was flying back then while McGeary and his colleagues seem to have used that weekend in Killarney as a bonding session and the result as a means of concentrating minds and recalibrating the tactics

(3) This victory means a lot to Cathal McShane, sharing the moment with his girlfriend Kaitlynn Coyle at the final whistle. In February last year he sustained a serious ankle injury that ruled him out for the rest of the 2020 season and he worked his way back to fitness only this summer

5 TG4 All-Ireland Ladies Junior Football Championship Final - Croke Park, Dublin
Wicklow 2-17   Antrim 1-09

TG4 All-Ireland Ladies Intermediate Football Championship Final - Croke Park, Dublin
Westmeath 4-19   Wexford 0-06

1.

2.

(1-2) The juniors are first into action in the ladies football All-Ireland finals day in Croke Park.
Wicklow's Clodagh Fox, who scored 1-3 on the day, gets out in front of Antrim's Duana Coleman
to make a fine catch and, afterwards, Sarah Jane Winders oversees the captain's ceremonial
honours by raising the West County Hotel Cup

(3-4) Beaming with pride, Westmeath captain Fiona Claffey raises the Mary Quinn Memorial
Cup after their massive victory in the ladies intermediate final while Wexford's Chloe Dwyer
feels the pain of defeat – some days it just doesn't run for you. Commenting on her 18th season
of intercounty football, Claffey said: "I've been around a while. One of the girls was one when
I started playing with Westmeath." That's commitment

4.

1.

2.

5 TG4 All-Ireland Ladies Senior Football Championship Final - Croke Park, Dublin
Dublin 0-12   Meath 1-11

3.

4.

(1) Running on to the green carpet. Meath take to the field for the senior final against Dublin on the biggest day in the Ladies Gaelic Football Association calendar. What's about to unfold is another seismic shock to the system

(2) Standing on the red carpet. The President of Ireland, Michael D Higgins, prepares to be introduced to the crowd now that Covid restrictions have been eased and presentation protocols for Croke Park fixtures can be resumed

(3) That goal. Emma Duggan lobs Ciara Trent after noticing the Dublin goalkeeper off her line for a sensational early goal for Meath, a crucial score in an absorbing contest. "Goal, of course," was Emma's answer when someone had the temerity to ask her whether she was going for a goal or a point

(4) A great hair day. Meath's Emma Troy manages to hang on to the ball under pressure from Lyndsey Davey of Dublin – and it's also a challenge for their ponytails

1.

2.

(1) Change of direction. Vikki Wall's ball-carrying skills were central to Meath's success and earned her the player of the match award. Here, Wall attempts to shrug off a tackle by Lauren Magee of Dublin

(2) The first one is special. Shauna Ennis becomes the first Meath woman to raise the Brendan Martin Cup skyward amid great scenes of celebration. This unlikely triumph for a team that won the intermediate championship last year ends the Dubs' quest for five consecutive senior titles

(3) As one. Silverware out in front and treated like Royalty at last, the Meath panel and backroom support lap up the moment in front of Hill 16. Their superb conditioning, defensive structure and counter-attacking style have paid off – all masterminded by manager Eamonn Murray, front left

" I never questioned that we would win. Not for one minute. We knew that this year we would win every game. So we didn't worry about an All-Ireland, didn't even think about it **"**

Meath manager Eamonn Murray describes how single-minded and focused his side were throughout 2021

3.

11 GAA Football All-Ireland Senior Championship Final - Croke Park, Dublin
Tyrone 2-14 Mayo 0-15

(1) When Tyrone turn up, they turn up. Joint managers Feargal Logan and Brian Dooher, left, lead their team towards the dressing-room on All-Ireland final day

(2) A lán spraoi. It's a question of priorities for Mayo supporter and Jones' Road resident Seán McKeown who tends to his lawn before the final

(3) Meanwhile on a much larger lawn across the road, Mayo head for their warm-up having posed for the traditional squad photo. The time to end the talking is fast approaching, now they need to finish the job having taken out Dublin in the semi-finals

1.

2.

"It was tight at times and the missed penalty was probably the big turning point in the game. The boys put in real effort and dug deep, gave everything they had to give, and in the end it got us over the line"

A delighted Tyrone joint manager Brian Dooher following the final whistle

3.

2.

(1) It's tense, it's tight and it's deadly serious. And that's just in the stands. Judging by these anxious faces among the 41,150 final-day attendance, following a close, exciting match is not everyone's idea of relaxation. Nor is a yearning for success after 70 years of heartbreak

(2) On his shoulder. In one of the many fascinating match-ups in the game, Tyrone captain Pádraig Hampsey keeps a close eye on Mayo forward Tommy Conroy as he wraps his right hand around the ball

1.

2.

3.

(1) Miss the penalty, pay the penalty. In this moment Mayo forward Ryan O'Donoghue knows how cruel sport can be as he watches his 40th-minute penalty shave Niall Morgan's left-hand post and drift inches wide. It's one of four missed goal chances by the Connacht champions – and they're costly

(2) Goals win games – Exhibit B. A double strike seals the deal and title number four for Tyrone. That man Cathal McShane repeats his semi-final offering with a flicked goal over the head of Mayo goalkeeper Rob Hennelly and Darren McCurry adopts a similar approach for their second goal. Crucial incidents that illustrate the difference between the teams

1.

2.

3.

4.

5.

6.

(1) Accepting the plaudits. Darren McCurry greets the final whistle after possibly his best season in a Tyrone jersey. The man they call the Dazzler contributed 1-4 in the final and was voted player of the match – hard to believe that he left the panel in 2018 and wasn't around when Tyrone contested that year's All-Ireland final

(2) Yards and parallel dimensions. Substitutes Ben McDonnell, left, and Darragh Canavan are ecstatic at the end of the game as Jordan Flynn, left, and Enda Hession get to grips with another final defeat for Mayo

(3) Satisfaction. Tyrone's Pádraig Hampsey joins the exclusive club of All-Ireland winning football captains. And doesn't it taste sweet

(4-5) Warriors and true sportsmen. Lee Keegan and Aidan O'Shea, who have been on the losing side in six All-Ireland finals, stay on the pitch out of respect for Tyrone. Keegan, who did his utmost to galvanise his Mayo colleagues, is in the company of his one-year-old daughter Líle while O'Shea puts his own disappointment aside to console Ryan O'Donoghue

(6) Clutching at Sam. After pulling off one of the greatest coups – a tactical masterplan – the jubilant Tyrone players pose for photographs as the trophy leaves the podium to join them pitch-side. The advice of joint manager Brian Dooher – "don't wait until tomorrow, do what you can today" – was certainly taken on board

11 GAA Football All-Ireland Senior Championship Final - Croke Park, Dublin
Tyrone 2-14 Mayo 0-15

1.

2.

3.

(1) A close-knit family. The great Peter Canavan, the former Tyrone All-Ireland winning captain and television pundit, chats with grand-daughter Ava and son-in-law Peter Harte after the final

(2) Heading for the Hill. The Tyrone players, led by Frank Burns with the coveted Sam Maguire Cup, march on a Hill 16 unadorned with the usual sky blue

(3) Delivering the title in their first year in charge, joint managers Brian Dooher and Feargal Logan toast the county's latest success. Dooher becomes only the 12th man in GAA history to win the All-Ireland as both player and manager and only the fifth – following Kevin Heffernan, Tony Hanahoe, Páidí Ó Sé and Billy Morgan – to do it as manager and captain

(4) A gentleman to the last. In the failing light and a near empty stadium, Mayo manager James Horan tries to explain how it all went wrong while his son Eoghan plays alongside him

❝ The performance wasn't what we are capable of. It's very disappointing, but as we have said after every game you cannot get too up or too down because of the result, just try and learn from it. We'll do the same again now ❞

A disappointed Mayo manager James Horan on another bitter All-Ireland final lesson for his county

12 All-Ireland Senior Camogie Championship Final - Croke Park, Dublin
Galway 1-15   Cork 1-12

" All the great teams did it back-to-back. I think that's the challenge now for this team. We probably need to win another All-Ireland if we want to be called a great team "
Galway manager Cathal Murray isn't slow about setting a target for his charges

1.

3.

(1) Possession comes dropping slow. Orlaith McGrath of Galway only has eyes for the sliotar as Cork's Pamela Mackey closes in during camogie All-Ireland finals day at Croke Park. Orlaith is one of three sisters on the winning panel alongside Siobhán, who scored their crucial goal, and Niamh

(2) Heading across the Shannon. Captain Sarah Dervan becomes the first Galway player to raise the O'Duffy Cup twice, a magical moment for the veteran who lifted the trophy in 2019 and whose involvement with the panel goes back to the 2008 loss to Cork

(3) Not to be. Cork's pacey full forward Amy O'Connor, understandably dejected, leaves the pitch afterwards. Perhaps thoughts are already turning to next year

Here's to the next quarter century

A season of sundays

1997 – 2021

Since it first hit the shelves all those years ago, A Season of Sundays, *Sportsfile's annual review of the Gaelic Games year, has been savoured and enjoyed by players, spectators and enthusiasts everywhere. Each issue is packed with vivid and memorable images that embrace the very heart and soul of Ireland's national games. For many it's the perfect bookend to the year. For our award-winning team of photographers it's a labour of love which, thanks to the support of our loyal readers and sponsors, we hope to continue for decades to come.*

sportsfile
PUBLISHING

Patterson House, 14 South Circular Road
Portobello, Dublin 8, D08 T3FK, Ireland

www.sportsfile.com